JO

"This Prayer Rain book is the most powerful Prayer Manual ever written for Startups & Entrepreneurs. You now have a true prayer guide to help you pray and achieve results. With faith, surely the answer you seek is at hand!"

PRAYER RAIN

BREAKTHROUGH
PRAYERS
for

STARTUPS &
ENTREPRENEURS

PRAYER RAIN: BREAKTHROUGH PRAYERS FOR STARTUPS & ENTREPRENEURS
by John Miller

CONTENTS

DEDICATION

This book is dedicated to anyone who has been inspired to start a new business. May God give you the blessing that will set you apart and make your business a resounding success.

BOOKS BY JOHN MILLER

THE LIFE OF JESUS CHRIST SERIES

1. **The Last Week of Jesus Christ:** The Full Gospel Account of the Death, Resurrection & Ascension of Jesus Christ (Available in both text-only and illustrated editions)

2. **Jesus Christ the Healer:** The Full Gospel Account of the Healing Miracles of Jesus Christ (Available in both text-only and illustrated editions)

3. **Jesus Christ the Deliverer:** The Full Gospel Account of the Deliverance Ministrations of Jesus Christ (Available in both text-only and illustrated editions)

4. **Jesus Christ the Miracle Worker:** The Full Gospel Account of the Miracles of Jesus Christ (Available in both text-only and illustrated editions)

5. **Jesus Christ the Storyteller:** The Full Gospel Account of the Parables & Spiritual Illustrations of Jesus Christ (Available in both text-only and illustrated editions)

COMMAND THE MORNING SERIES

1. Command the Morning: 2015 Daily Prayer Manual

2. Command the Morning: 2015 Daily Prayer Manual for

Business Owners
3. Command the Morning: 2015 Daily Prayer Manual for Working People
4. Command the Morning: 2015 Daily Prayer Manual for Single Men
5. Command the Morning: 2015 Daily Prayer Manual for Single Women
6. Command the Morning: 2015 Daily Prayer Manual for Husbands and Fathers
7. Command the Morning: 2015 Daily Prayer Manual for Wives and Mothers
8. Command the Morning: 2015 Daily Prayer Manual for The Family
9. Command the Morning: 2015 Daily Prayer Manual for Students

PRAY YOUR WAY SERIES

1. Pray Your Way Into 2015
2. Pray Your Way Into 2015 for Single Men
3. Pray Your Way Into 2015 for Single Women
4. Pray Your Way Into 2015 for Married Men
5. Pray Your Way Into 2015 for Married Women
6. Pray Your Way Into 2015 for Students

OPEN HEAVENS SERIES

PRAYER RAIN SERIES

For newer books visit,
www.amazon.com/author/johnmillerbooks

INTRODUCTION

If you are an entrepreneur and you are about to start a new business, you need to seek the face of the Lord. On one hand, there are millions of businesses across the world that are begun without divine guidance and regardless of the capital invested and the technical knowhow of their founders, millions of these businesses ultimately fail. On the other hand, there are entrepreneurs who genuinely seek God's face before they start their businesses and those businesses not only stand the test of time but grow to become highly profitable. The difference between these two types of businesses is the Blessing of the Almighty.

If you are interested in seeking God's help for your new business, this book "Prayer Rain: Breakthrough Prayers For Startups & Entrepreneurs" is what you need. Every single chapter was written to enable you achieve one thing - a profitable business.

In Chapter 1 "The Reality of Starting A New Business", we take a quick look at what starting a new business means for entrepreneurs. What will it cost me to be an entrepreneur? Can I succeed? All these and more questions are answered.

In Chapter 2, we answer an age-long question. The question "when will God answer my prayers?" This chapter provides you with everything you can do to get quick answers to your prayers and what may cause a delay in the answer you are seeking.

In Chapter 3, you are exposed to all the things you need to do in order to be qualified to receive an answer to your prayer. This chapter is so crucial and vital. Please do not skip this chapter and ensure you do everything therein if you want to receive an answer from heaven. In Chapter 4, we teach you how to prepare for the prayers you are about to pray. Like chapter 3, this is a requirement for finding success with this book. Read the chapter thoroughly and do everything stated therein.

Chapter 5 is the main focus of this book. It contains all the prayers you need to pray to get your business on the path to maximum profitability.

Without a doubt, if you do everything that is written in this book and you have faith, you will prosper in your startup and your journey as an entrepreneur will be a success by the Power in the mighty name of Jesus.

Your friend-in-Christ,
John Miller

PRAYER RAIN: BREAKTHROUGH PRAYERS FOR STARTUPS & ENTREPRENEURS

1

THE REALITY OF STARTING A NEW BUSINESS

1. Before you start a business, make sure that you have a curious and creative mind.

2. Assess yourself to ensure that you have a natural, in-born desire to make money.

3. As far as your startup solves a real-world problem or satisfies a need for a good number of people, your age or background does not matter.

4. You must have a natural desire to trade. That is, to buy and sell.

5. Make sure your desire to do business is so strong that you wake up with it and you sleep with it. And during your waking hours, make it paramount on your mind.

6. Though not necessary, you should have a history of doing some kind of business, even if this means just selling to friends and relatives.

7. If you have done some business in the past, it means you may or may not have a history of silly business ventures and silly expenditures. These kinds of experiences happen to most entrepreneurs especially at the beginning.

8. Becoming an entrepreneur is not rocket science. However, at the very minimum, an ability to read, write and calculate is thoroughly essential for startup success.

9. You must have the ability to objectively learn from and move beyond past errors, mistakes and business misadventures.

10. When you are new in business, there are people who are always ready to scam, cheat and deceive you. This includes even people you have trusted and looked up to for guidance for years. You need to be very careful so you don't suffer unnecessary loss.

11. Your success or otherwise in business can determine who you will marry and who you marry can determine the success of your business. This is called the business and marriage cycle.

12. You must be willing to do the research necessary to understand the fundamentals of the business you want to go into. This might include reading books, online research, using the phone and email to ask

questions, attending expos, exhibitions and trade fairs and other such ways to get the information you need to make the right decisions.

13. Expect your family to be angry with (or at best worried for) you when you announce to them that you want to do business instead of looking for a job. This is where your previous history in doing business can serve to either encourage or discourage them. If you have had some business success in the past, they might not be so worried and might even support you. However, if you have failed in the past, do not be surprised if their support is not readily forthcoming.

14. You need to seek God's face regarding the business you want to do.

15. You must be willing to go anywhere possible to get answers to all your questions regarding your business of interest.

16. Sometimes the answers to your questions might lie with people younger than you are or belonging to a social class lower than yours or not as intelligent as you are. However, since they have the knowledge and the answers and you do not, you must humble yourself to get what you want.

17. You must also be willing to pay for information either through books, audio and video products, online

webinars, physical seminars and conferences, etc.

18. You must be willing to sweat. You have to be willing to roll up your sleeves and use the knowledge you have assembled to do actual work that will result in a viable product.

19. You must be willing and mentally prepared to experiment over and over again until your product or service is ready for the public.

20. You must accept the fact that you will fail. In fact, sometimes you will fail several times. Therefore, you must never be discouraged by failure and you must try over and over again until your product or service offering is excellent. Very few people get it right the first time. And even if they do, each month or each year, they keep improving their product or service. You should know that all the big names you are familiar with and probably look up to failed on their first attempt. Failure is just a fact of life.

21. Becoming an entrepreneur means, at least for a while, you might have to sacrifice certain things. Things like relationships, vacations and non-essential trips, school (especially or only if your startup is tackling a once-in-a-lifetime opportunity), etc., all might be sacrificed so that you can completely focus on the task that you have at hand.

22. You must have people that are close to you - friends, family members and other relatives, employees, etc., who can help you test or assess your product or service without familial bias. This initial testing is to give you feedback on whether or not your offering has sufficient quality or not before you put it out in the market. This is very important. Never sell a product or service that has not been thoroughly tested.

23. You must be willing to start small with regard to the scale of your operations. For example, at the beginning, instead of building or buying an office, consider renting to save your money.

24. At the beginning, if you are not able to afford salaries, you need to properly articulate your vision to friends and relatives who are available but cautious about helping you. If your vision is not clear or it doesn't look or sound interesting or convincing enough, they will probably turn you down. Note that if this happens, the workload might overwhelm you and this might affect your business.

25. You must be willing to endure ridicule or shame from detractors, friends, relatives, co-workers, etc., who do not understand your vision or have access to the facts you have researched. Do not let ridicule prevent you from achieving your vision. Keep going.

26. You need to have reasons for pursuing the business you are in and you must set goals regarding the business. These goals and reasons must always be on your mind and in your memory so that in times of discouragement and pressure to quit, you will always remember exactly why you embarked on the venture in the first place.

27. Your startup must give world-class customer service.

28. You must market your product or service otherwise nobody will know about it.

29. Your marketing efforts must be sustained otherwise it will soon fade from people's memories and consciousness.

30. You must always have a pen and notebook or the digital equivalent (such as the Onenote app installed on your mobile device) with you at all times. This is necessary to record ideas that can come to you anywhere and at anytime. When you have an idea, do not rely on your ability to always recollect it. Remember, there are other ideas in the queue that can knock off all previous ideas you've had. Again, write down all your ideas.

31. Do price research. Make sure that your product or service is not the most expensive amongst others in its range. Let your pricing be appropriate.

32. When you first introduce your product to the public, despite your best efforts, it is possible that it might not sell at all in the beginning or at best, it might get very low patronage. If your research was/is sound and you are confident of the fundamentals of the business, do not be discouraged.

33. In fact, it is possible that other similar products in your field might be selling while yours isn't. Do not be discouraged.

34. Again, if your research is sound and in fact, if others in the same business appear to be prospering, you need to find out why you are not especially by researching why they are. You need to be totally objective about the process. You might find, for example, that the problem is that you are in the wrong location.

35. If your business is a physical business with physical goods or services that require human-to-human contact, you must ensure that your business is strategically located so as to ensure maximum exposure to customers.

36. Make sure you do detailed research on what the best location for your business is for your particular kind of business.

37. Read, read and re-read any contract you are required

to sign in the course of doing business. This is essential so that you do not jeopardize yourself or the future of your business. If you can afford to, try to get a lawyer to read through contracts for you. But even if you do this, you still need to read and understand the contract for yourself and then ask your lawyer any question that comes to mind. This way you have a comprehensive view of what you are committing yourself to and whether or not you want to commit.

38. On your own part, make sure when necessary to draw up agreements and contracts, then require anyone doing business with you to sign. If necessary and if you can afford to, get a lawyer to do this for you. If you cannot, a written agreement stating the terms as well as conditions and dates might suffice. Doing this is necessary for your own protection especially in today's world where integrity is becoming a scarce commodity.

39. Make sure that your product is the best available of its kind and make sure that people can afford it.

40. If you are just starting out and you appear to be making great success, you might be tempted to expand and open as many branches as possible of your business so as to have maximum sales. Please note that you should be careful not to do this too fast. What works in one place might not work in another. That said, as profit is usually the main reason for

doing business, if you have done your research and you are sure that it is sound and it is telling you that expansion is good for you, before you act, seek God's final approval through prayer.

41. Sometimes your success might have a negative effect on other people who might not necessarily be your competitors. For example, if you start a new school business and it's turning out great, it is possible that you will have lots of parents with vehicles parking in front of the gates of your neighbors when dropping off or picking up their kids. This traffic buildup on the street can block your neighbors from coming out or going into their own homes. In order not to attract animosity and resentment which might result in confrontations, you need to be wise in handling these types of situations. If confrontations ensue, it could have a deleterious effect on your business. If however you seek counsel and handle the matter wisely, it would be a win-win for everyone - your neighbors, your customers and yourself.

42. Be totally honest. Never give or take bribes and never be tempted to be fraudulent. Breaking through when you are 100% honest might take some time in a corrupt world BUT when you do it would be breakthrough built on a solid foundation. In addition, by being honest in all your dealings, you will never have to worry that one day, somebody somewhere will expose you, disgrace you and bring your name

and business to ruin.

43. Sometimes, the authorities (for example, industry regulators, landlords, etc) might force you to close down your business for one reason or the other. No matter how heart-wrenching this might be, do not give up.

44. If you have debts, it is possible that your home or other property might be foreclosed on by entities that have lent you money. As sad as this event might be, if you are sure that your research is sound and other people are succeeding in that business, remain persistent and do not let the loss of your property sidetrack you.

45. On a personal note, if your business is not succeeding as quickly as it should, your fiancé or fiancee might dump you. And if you are married, your spouse might threaten to divorce you. But you have to keep at it if you know you are on the right track.

46. If your business is not succeeding as quickly as it should, it can lead to depression. But you have to keep at it.

47. Again, you might feel like a complete loser and a failure in life, if your startup is not making money as it should.

48. You might feel that your life is stagnant or worse, retrogressing, especially when you see your friends and relatives "making it" - buying property, traveling around the world, etc.

49. Business ideas that lead to breakthrough can come from anybody, anywhere and at anytime of the day.

50. You need to be alert and discerning to be able to recognize when you are encountering the idea that will turn your life around.

51. When you need to solve a business problem and you approach the recognized expert in that field to help you solve that problem, make sure you have all your facts ready before meeting with the expert. This is important so as to save everyone's time and more importantly so that you would be taken seriously and given the attention your matter deserves. The opposite will happen if you go to such a meeting unprepared.

52. When you approach an expert concerning your business problem, cast aside all fear and nervousness and get past the shyness if you have any. Remember why you are there. Give it to him or her as it is with all the respect and confidence you can muster. The solution you are seeking is necessary for your business to succeed, so make sure you get it.

53. Do not be shy about or ashamed of changing your line of business if necessary. Government legislation, a shift in demographics, the passage of time or other reasons can cause your current business to lose its erstwhile viability. If there is a solid, infallible issue affecting the viability of your current business, use all the rules so far covered to conceive and settle on a new business and move on with your life. For example, if you were selling typewriters in the 1980s and 1990s, it would be silly in this day and age not to drop that business and pick up something else to sell like computers, tablets or smartphones. The only exception to do this example, is if you are a collector and seller of vintage items.

54. Do detailed supplier research. If your business requires raw materials, make sure you do proper research to ensure whomever will be your supplier will not scam you of your hard-earned money. Please ensure that their raw materials are not only the best available but also the most competitively priced. You should also ask "what supplier does the competitor use?" as well as "is there anyone better than that supplier?" Do your detailed supplier research.

55. When recruiting employees, amongst other things, endeavor not to recruit "Yes Men/Women" employees. This kind of people are very dangerous because they will never disagree with you. Out of the fear of offending you and losing their job, they will be

afraid to speak their minds and offer suggestions or opinions that might help move the business forward. On the other hand, do not recruit employees who will always disagree with you, criticize your decisions and question your authority especially before other employees. Such employees can cause division in your company. Please get employees with the right constitution.

56. Never be afraid to go to any city or country where the materials you need for your product or service can be sourced at the best quality for the best price.

57. Always make sure you are credit-worthy at all times. You never know when this will come in handy.

58. You must set aside funds for experiments and tests. As we have seen, failure is almost a must at the beginning of product or service development. If you do not have the funds for experiments and tests for your products, your company might die at this stage and the product might never see the light of day despite the promise it holds.

59. Be prepared to do these experiments night and day until you get a finished, high quality product ready for the marketplace.

60. Sometimes, money pressure might lead you to sell your personal property to pursue success in your

business. In this case, note that there is nothing prayer cannot do.

61. In your quest to become an entrepreneur, depending on your line of business, there will be times when the weather might appear to be conspiring against you and your business. For example, it might rain when you do not want and not rain when you want it to. God can help in instances like these.

62. While you are working on your new business with all of its pressures, you are not immune from problems that affect every other human being. For example, issues concerning your family members can come up. For example, a relative can fall sick, some may die. In times like these, you might feel that there is something out to get you or get your business. Whether or not this is the case, do not give up.

63. When doing your experiments and tests, make sure to keep notes. This way you will remember what works and what doesn't. Notes are important because they prevent you from repeating the same mistakes over and over. More importantly, they are necessary as guides to provide you with the information to repeat the pathway to products or services when necessary. Make sure to store your notes very carefully.

64. Throughout history, men and women have made discoveries which only became obvious to them by

accident. Some of these discoveries have led to multi-billion dollar businesses. Think of the accidental discovery of penicillin. You need to pray for positive accidents of this sort to happen to you and from which you can get your turning point breakthrough.

65. Once you have your solid, finished product and probably before you start advertising, you need to think of distribution. If you sell a physical item, like packaged software on discs or packaged snacks for example, you should look for a company with a chain of several stores that you can distribute to. Companies like this can centrally purchase your products and then distribute them on a regional, national and sometimes intercontinental basis to their network of stores. This approach will give you maximum visibility and profitability. The same principle applies to businesses selling digital items like ebooks and downloadable software, If you choose a good distributor, they will make sure your item is available, on a worldwide basis, to all the relevant stores.

66. If your product is completely new, prepare to be underestimated by some distributors. But never let this get you down. At the distributing company, make sure you get the person or entity in a position of authority to try out your product by themselves so that they can act quickly on your behalf.

67. Pursuing your business might mean waiting in office receptions and waiting rooms of clients or distributors for several hours, days, weeks or months without anyone attending to you. You might be told that the person in a position of authority over your matter is in a meeting, is sick or on a holiday and all manner of excuses. But never let all these get to you. Make sure your voice is heard and get them to at least try your product out by themselves.

68. Whenever you are in a place for a purpose relating to your business, always make sure to know all the rules of that place so that you will not be delayed or disqualified in any way. Make this a priority. Get all necessary documentation on the place and master all the policies.

69. Design and packaging are important. Whether your product or service is physical or digital, it must meet certain design requirements and at the same time appeal to customers. The packaging of physical goods must meet requirements of distributors. Policies on product size [for proper display on store shelves], packaging type, color, etc. must be adhered to. Same goes for digital items, ebook cover size, instruction on splash screen sizes for mobile apps, etc. must be adhered to. Do not try to be innovative in this regard. Let your innovation be in the product itself not in adhering to rules for its distribution.

70. Ensure that your pricing satisfies the distributor for the category or type of your product. Keep in mind that in addition to your own profit, the distributor also needs to make its own profit while thinking of the cost implications for the customer. So price your items appropriately if you are using a distributor.

71. During your trying times in business, it is good to have someone who believes in you. He or she can help to re-affirm to you that you will succeed. However, if you have no such person and cannot get such a person, this book will have to suffice.

72. If you cannot handle the design or packaging of your product by yourself, make sure you get an expert to do it for you. Give the expert your ideas and brainstorm together on the best outcome for your product.

73. When your product is to be or has been submitted for distribution approval, you need to pray. Submitting an application for distribution does not guarantee it will be granted to you. Consider that if your application is rejected, your product will not get the regional, national or intercontinental distribution you are seeking, which will be a disaster especially if there is no alternative. Therefore, prayer at this stage is crucial.

74. Even if your product meets all criteria set by some

distributors, they might still reject it for any reason. Take the rejection in your stride. After all, you are not the first person to be rejected and you will not be the last. However, ask the distributor questions on why it was rejected, get the answers, address their concerns and then try again and keep trying till you get in.

75. If after several attempts a distributor refuses to take your product, it might be time to try another distributor, if such exists. That said, there are prayers you can pray to avoid rejection of this sort. Such prayers can enable you get favor before any approval agent or board so that you can prosper.

76. Repeated rejections of a product you have spent all your money on can lead to severe depression. Some people think of the consequences of the rejection (which can include bankruptcy) and therefore sink into depression and everything associated with that - including thoughts of suicide. Remember, whether you believe it or not, any man or woman that takes a life (whether yours or another's) will end up in hell fire. I assure you that one second in hell fire is incomparable to 1,000 lifetimes of product rejection. No problem on earth is worth a second, not to talk of an eternity in hell. Never consider this as an option. Keep working.

77. There have been instances of chance breakthroughs recorded in history. Someone somewhere notices

your product and tries it out. Then suddenly, you get a phone call or an email asking you to bring your products to certain places which can distribute them worldwide. You can pray for this sort of breakthrough to happen to you.

78. Certain distributors have certain equipment requirements. You must do your best to fulfill these requirements otherwise your product might be rejected. FCertain distributors have certain equipment requirements. You must do your best to fulfill these requirements otherwise your product might be rejected. For example, it is commonly known that if you want to submit an app into the Apple Mac app store or the iOS app store, you need to have a machine running Mac OS X. In the same vein, if you want to distribute an edible product for instance, you must have everything in place to pass factory or premises inspections from government and chain store officials. And you need to pray for favor to pass these inspections. You need to meet and exceed all requirements.

79. Each day when you wake up, you need to look at yourself in the mirror and affirm to yourself that you are great and that you will make it in this life. Declare to yourself that doors will open to you and you will get your breakthrough and prosper.

80. On the day that your physical or digital item gets

approval, give thanks to the Almighty. After this, begin the work of marketing your item. Let all the world know about your fantastic new product and service. When success comes, do not forget to remain humble. Pride goes before a fall.

2

WHEN WILL GOD ANSWER MY PRAYERS?

For most people who decide to turn to God to seek for a solution to their problems, one question that is paramount on their minds is: when exactly will God answer my prayer? The answer to this question is the focus of this chapter.

For every child of God, with regard to the timing of an answer from heaven in reply to your prayer, there are two types of prayers:

1. Prayers that receive immediate answers
2. Prayers whose answers are delayed

1. PRAYERS THAT RECEIVE IMMEDIATE ANSWERS

When you pray, you can receive answers immediately. The Bible is filled with people who prayed and received immediate answers from heaven. The following four examples illustrate this:

A) Immediate Answer To Prayer For Assurance of Eternal Life

The bible reveals to us that on the day Jesus was being crucified and he was about to give up the ghost, he had two other persons with him who were criminals and unlike Jesus actually deserved to die based on their deeds and the law. If they had died as they were, both would have gone to hell. But one of them acted wisely, said a simple and short prayer and got an immediate answer from the son of the living God.

Luke 23:39-43: "One of the criminals who hung there hurled insults at him: "Aren't you the Messiah? Save yourself and us!" But the other criminal rebuked him. "Don't you fear God," he said, "since you are under the same sentence? We are punished justly, for we are getting what our deeds deserve. But this man has done nothing wrong." **Then he said, "Jesus, remember me when you come into your kingdom."** Jesus *answered* him, *'Truly I tell you, today you will be with me in paradise.'"*

B) Immediate Answer To Prayer From Praying and Singing

There is another very remarkable instance in the book of Acts in the Bible that properly illustrates people receiving instant answers to their prayers.

Paul and Silas had travelled to Philippi, a Roman colony to preach the gospel. While there, a demon-possessed slave woman started following them about, making certain pronouncements concerning them. The pronouncements though true became unbearable to the men and so one day Paul, being fed up, turned to the woman and said "*In the name of Jesus Christ I command you to come out of her!*" and instantly the demon left her.

This is the first instance of immediate answer to their prayer.

In the second instance, unbeknownst to them, the owners of the slave-woman had been making money from her prophetic abilities. Now that the spirit had left her, they were very angry. They took Paul and Silas to court and lied against them with the support of a mob. The two men were stripped naked, severe flogged and deposited in the inner cell of a prison where they were tied down and placed under armed guard.

The above situation looks like a hopeless situation. But at midnight, something happened.

Acts 16:25-31: "About midnight Paul and Silas were *praying and singing hymns to God*, and the other prisoners were listening to them. *Suddenly* there was such a violent earthquake that the foundations of the prison were shaken. At once all the prison doors flew open, and everyone's chains came loose. The jailer woke up, and when he saw the prison doors open, he drew his sword and was about to kill himself because he thought the prisoners had escaped. But Paul shouted, "Don't harm yourself! We are all here!" The jailer called for lights, rushed in and fell trembling before Paul and Silas. He then brought them out and asked, 'Sirs, what must I do to be saved?' They replied, 'Believe in the Lord Jesus, and you will be saved—you and your household.'"

In this second instance, Paul and Silas combined praying with singing and got an immediate answer to the problem they had at hand - freedom from unjustified bondage. As singing was pivotal in this example, Chapter

4 contains songs that you need to sing before beginning the actual prayers in the final chapter. Please do not skip this chapter under any circumstance.

C) Immediate Answer To Prayer From Issuing Commands To Anything Made By God

At a point in the history of Israel when Joshua was its leader, the country was involved in many wars. Kingdoms that did not want to be destroyed by the jewish army would sign peace treaties. One of such kingdoms was Gibeon, which was very prosperous.

Unknown to the people of Gibeon, the king of a rival kingdom, King Adoni-Zedek of Jerusalem managed to form an accord with the Kings of Hebron, Jarmuth, Lachish and Eglon. Their focus was the destruction of Gibeon. As they besieged Gibeon, the Gibeonites sent word to Joshua saying "Do not abandon your servants. Come up to us quickly and save us! Help us, because all the Amorite kings from the hill country have joined forces against us."

Joshua in response, honored his treaty and after receiving assurance from the Lord, marched with his army to save Gibeon. With the aid of divine intervention from God, they began to defeat Adoni-Zedek and his cohorts. But as night approached, Joshua was concerned that the task might not be completed and so he did something no man had ever done before.

Joshua 10:12-15: "On the day the Lord gave the Amorites over to Israel, Joshua said to the Lord in the presence of Israel: 'Sun, stand still over Gibeon, and you, moon, over the Valley of Aijalon.' *So the sun stood still and the moon stopped*, till the nation avenged itself on its enemies, as it is written in the Book of Jashar. The sun stopped in the middle of the sky and delayed going down about a full day. There has never been a day like it before or since, a day when the Lord listened to a human being. Surely the Lord was fighting for Israel! Then Joshua returned with all Israel to the camp at Gilgal."

Joshua commanded the sun and the moon to stand still and God granted his request immediately because it was expedient.

D) Immediate Answer To Prayer From Request By Faith To God To Prove Himself

The final example of immediate answer to prayer leads us to the Prophet Elijah in the Bible. In the book of I Kings, the King of Israel, Ahab had been completely dominated by his wife, Jezebel so much so that he turned his heart away from the Lord and began the worship of Baal. He had also employed prophets from all over Israel to administer the worship of Baal. As Elijah was a man of God and could not take this, he became a thorn in Ahab's flesh and the King had been looking for him to the extent that there was no kingdom at the time that he had not sent people to go hunt for Elijah.

Finally, Elijah showed up in Israel determined to demonstrate once and for all that there was only one God - the Almighty God. On the day Elijah re-surfaced, he met Obadiah, the King's palace administrator on the way and told him to go inform Ahab that he was back and he wanted to see him. Though Obadiah worked for Ahab, he remained devoted to God. Despite this however, he protested heavily against Elijah's request. He was afraid Elijah might not turn up and as a result, Ahab would have him killed for exciting him unnecessarily with a lie. Can you blame Obadiah?

I Kings 18:15-24: "Elijah said, 'As the Lord Almighty lives, whom I serve, I will surely present myself to Ahab today'. So Obadiah went to meet Ahab and told him, and Ahab went to meet Elijah. When he saw Elijah, he said to him, 'Is that you, you troubler of Israel?' 'I have not made trouble for Israel,' Elijah replied. 'But you and your father's family have. You have abandoned the Lord's commands and have followed the Baals. Now summon the people from all over Israel to meet me on Mount Carmel. And bring the four hundred and fifty prophets of Baal and the four hundred prophets of Asherah, who eat at Jezebel's table.'

So Ahab sent word throughout all Israel and assembled the prophets on Mount Carmel. Elijah went before the people and said, 'How long will you waver between two opinions? If the Lord is God, follow him; but if Baal is God, follow him.' But the people said nothing.

Then Elijah said to them, 'I am the only one of the Lord's prophets left, but Baal has four hundred and fifty prophets. Get two bulls for us. Let Baal's prophets choose one for themselves, and let them cut it into pieces and put it on the wood but not set fire to it. I will prepare the other bull and put it on the wood but not set fire to it.

Then you call on the name of your god, and I will call on the name of the Lord. The god who answers by fire—he is God.' Then all the people said, What you say is good.'"

1 Kings 18-25-29: "Elijah said to the prophets of Baal, 'Choose one of the bulls and prepare it first, since there are so many of you. Call on the name of your god, but do not light the fire.' So they took the bull given them and prepared it. Then they called on the name of Baal from morning till noon. 'Baal, answer us!' they shouted. But there was no response; no one answered. And they danced around the altar they had made. At noon Elijah began to taunt them. 'Shout louder!' he said. 'Surely he is a god! Perhaps he is deep in thought, or busy, or traveling. Maybe he is sleeping and must be awakened.' So they shouted louder and slashed themselves with swords and spears, as was their custom, until their blood flowed. Midday passed, and they continued their frantic prophesying until the time for the evening sacrifice. But there was no response, no one answered, no one paid attention."

1 Kings 18:30-35: "Then Elijah said to all the people, 'Come here to me.' They came to him, and he repaired the altar of the Lord, which had been torn down. Elijah took twelve stones, one for each of the tribes descended from Jacob, to whom the word of the Lord had come, saying, 'Your name shall be Israel.' With the stones he built an altar in the name of the Lord, and he dug a trench around it large enough to hold two seahs of seed. He arranged the wood, cut the bull into pieces and laid it on the wood. Then he said to them, 'Fill four large jars

with water and pour it on the offering and on the wood.' 'Do it again,' he said, and they did it again. 'Do it a third time,' he ordered, and they did it the third time. The water ran down around the altar and even filled the trench."

1 Kings 18:30-35: "At the time of sacrifice, the prophet Elijah stepped forward and prayed: 'Lord, the God of Abraham, Isaac and Israel, let it be known today that you are God in Israel and that I am your servant and have done all these things at your command. *Answer me, Lord, answer me, so these people will know that you, Lord, are God*, and that you are turning their hearts back again.' *Then the fire of the Lord fell and burned up the sacrifice, the wood, the stones and the soil, and also licked up the water in the trench*. When all the people saw this, they fell prostrate and cried, 'The Lord—he is God! The Lord—he is God!'"

You can see from the passage that Baal embarrassed his prophets - they did their best to call him but there was no answer. On the contrary, when Elijah called on God to demonstrate his power, the Almighty answered immediately! Elijah had great faith and he was certain in his heart that God would do it. There was no other option. If there was no answer that day, Elijah would have been killed.

Clearly, there are prayers that you pray and for which you receive immediate answers and immediate manifestation.

2. PRAYERS WITH DELAYED ANSWERS

When you pray, you can also get delayed answers
Delayed answers can be attributed to any of the following:

a) Spiritual Obstruction
b) Misalignment of Faith
c) Inappropriate Timing
d) Lack of Fasting
e) Presence of Sin

A) Delayed Answers Resulting From Spiritual Obstruction

There was a time in the Bible when the children of Israel were taken captive by the Babylonians. The prophet Jeremiah prophesied that the captivity would last for seventy years only. However, when seventy years had expired, nothing appeared to be happening. Daniel became very worried and decided to pray to the Almighty about their freedom from captivity.

Daniel 10:2-3: "At that time I, Daniel, mourned for three weeks. I ate no choice food; no meat or wine touched my lips; and I used no lotions at all until the three weeks were over."

Twenty one days after Daniel began his prayer, a strange visitor paid him a visit.

Daniel 10:4-6: "On the twenty-fourth day of the first month, as I was standing on the bank of the great river, the Tigris, I looked up and there before me was a man dressed in linen, with a belt of fine gold from Uphaz around his waist. His body was like topaz, his face like lightning, his eyes like flaming torches, his arms and legs like the gleam of burnished bronze, and his voice like the sound of a multitude."

Daniel 10:12-14: "Then he continued, 'Do not be afraid, Daniel. Since the first day that you set your mind to gain understanding and to humble yourself before your God, your words were heard, and I have come in response to them. But the prince of the Persian kingdom resisted me twenty-one days. Then Michael, one of the chief princes, came to help me, because I was detained there with the king of Persia. Now I have come to explain to you what will happen to your people in the future...'"

From the passage, the angel clearly stated that Daniel's prayer was heard on the first day and he was dispatched to deliver the answer. However, a principality or spiritual being called the "Prince of Persia" resisted him on his way to the earth. Not only that, the place where the angel was detained was controlled by another spiritual entity called the "King of Persia". Not until Michael, a chief prince in heaven, came to his rescue could the angel deliver the answer to Daniel's prayer.

This amazingly revealing passage in scripture clearly shows that our prayers can be obstructed by spirit beings and spiritual forces.

What Do You Do If You Suspect The Answers To Your Prayers Are Being Spiritually Obstructed?

The wise thing to do is to do exactly what Daniel did that eventually got him his answer:

1. Read and re-read the above verses

2. Remind God of these verses and how He answered Daniel
3. Trust Him totally
4. Stand sure in faith that He will answer your prayer
5. Do not for any reason stop praying or believing

Romans 12:12: "Rejoice in hope, be patient in tribulation, be constant in prayer." Friend, if Daniel had stopped praying or believing, it is possible that the angel could have returned back to heaven without delivering the answer he was seeking. Do as Daniel did and wait on the Lord.

B) Delayed Answers Resulting From Misalignment of Faith

Hebrews 11:6: "And without faith it is impossible to please God, because anyone who comes to him must believe that He exists and that He rewards those who earnestly seek him."

Matthew 18:9: "Again, truly I tell you that if two of you on earth agree about anything they ask for, it will be done for them by my Father in heaven."

In order to get an answer to your prayer from God, it is necessary that you demonstrate faith. If you do not have faith, you cannot get any answer from God. Moreover, if the answer you are seeking involves the participation in one way or another of someone apart from yourself, in order to produce results, Matthew 18:9 says both of you stand a better chance of getting your prayer answered if you 'agree' and pray together. The word 'Agree' here amongst other things connotes deciding on what to pray on and having complete faith that the person you are praying to will provide a solution. In order words, both of you must have an alignment of your requests and faith. If not, there might be a delay or denial of the answer to your prayer.

The best way to develop faith is to read the Bible and listen to Christian sermons and messages. Romans 10:17 "So then faith comes by hearing, and hearing by the word of God."

Why is it important for the faith of the people involved to be aligned? There is an important story in the Bible about the inability of Abraham and Sarah to have children. God had told Abraham directly several years earlier that he would be the father of many nations and that he would bear a son called Isaac. And so, because he heard directly from the Lord, he had great faith that the son would come.

Sarah on the other hand, did not hear directly from God. What she heard was second-hand information as told to her by Abraham. Therefore, she had doubts and in fact, she had given up completely.

Eventually Sarah turned ninety while Abraham became one hundred years old. Naturally, at their age, all reproductive systems would have been long dead and become like fossils. However, one day, just as with Daniel, Abraham and Sarah received three strange visitors.

Genesis 18:1-2: "The Lord appeared to Abraham near the great trees of Mamre while he was sitting at the entrance to his tent in the heat of the day. Abraham looked up and saw three men standing nearby. When he saw them, he hurried from the entrance of his tent to meet them and bowed low to the ground."

Genesis 18:9-14: "'Where is your wife Sarah?' they asked him. 'There, in the tent,' he said. Then one of them said, 'I will surely return to you about this time next year, and Sarah your wife will have a son.' Now Sarah was listening at the entrance to the tent, which was behind him. Abraham and Sarah were already very old, and Sarah was past the age of childbearing. So Sarah laughed to herself as she thought, 'After I am worn out and my lord is old, will I now have this pleasure?' Then the Lord said to Abraham, 'Why did Sarah laugh and say, "Will I really have a child, now that I am old?" Is anything too hard for the Lord? I will return to you at the appointed time next year, and Sarah will have a son.'"

For the first time, Sarah heard the word of God directly herself and this activated her faith. Now, finally it became possible for both her and Abraham to agree in faith that the birth of their son would surely happen.

Genesis 21:1-7: "Now the Lord was gracious to Sarah as he had said, and the Lord did for Sarah what he had promised. Sarah became pregnant and bore a son to Abraham in his old age, at the very time God had promised him. Abraham gave the name Isaac to the son Sarah bore him... Abraham was a hundred years old when his son Isaac was born to him. Sarah said, 'God has brought me laughter, and everyone who hears about this will laugh with me.' And she added, 'Who would have said to Abraham that Sarah would nurse children? Yet I have borne him a son in his old age.'"

What Do You Do If You Suspect The Answers To Your Prayers Are Being Delayed Due To Misalignment of Faith?

As earlier mentioned, if the answer you are seeking involves the participation in one way or another of someone apart from yourself, in order to produce results, both of you stand a better chance of getting your prayer answered if you 'agree' and pray together.

Also, faith, which is the main ingredient in your agreement comes by reading and hearing the word of God. Ensure that christian materials in the area of your need are never scarce in your household. They will help you build the faith you need to receive expedited answers.

C) Delayed Answers Resulting From Inappropriate Timing

Ecclesiastes 3:1-8 "There is a time for everything, and a season for every activity under the heavens:
a time to be born and a time to die,
a time to plant and a time to uproot,
a time to kill and a time to heal,
a time to tear down and a time to build,
a time to weep and a time to laugh,
a time to mourn and a time to dance,
a time to scatter stones and a time to gather them,
a time to embrace and a time to refrain from embracing,

a time to search and a time to give up,

a time to keep and a time to throw away,

a time to tear and a time to mend,

a time to be silent and a time to speak,

a time to love and a time to hate, a time for war and a time for peace."

If in God's infinite wisdom, it is not yet time for your prayers to be answered, you will perceive such a situation as a delay.

Zechariah and Elizabeth had been married for years. Both were already advanced in years but the marriage had failed to produce a child. One can only imagine how many nights Elizabeth would have wet her bed with tears praying that God should give her a child, any child, male or female. Zechariah, who was a priest and as such a popular man, must have felt ashamed that he could not have a child. As a priest, one can only imagine how many times he would prayed over the years for a child with no answer of any sort. Nevertheless both husband and wife having accepted their fate in life remained righteous in the sight of God, observing all the Lord's commands and decrees blamelessly. Until one day - the appropriate time.

Luke 1:8-17: "Once when Zechariah's division was on duty and he was serving as priest before God, he was chosen by lot, according to the custom of the priesthood, to go into the temple of the Lord and burn incense. And when the time for the burning of incense came, all the assembled worshipers were praying outside. Then an angel of the Lord appeared to him, standing at the right side of the altar of incense. When Zechariah saw him, he was startled and was gripped with fear. But the angel said to him: 'Do not be afraid, Zechariah; *your prayer has been heard.* Your wife Elizabeth will bear you a son, and you are to call him John. He will be a joy and delight to you, and many will rejoice because of his birth, for he will be great in the sight of the Lord... He will bring back many of the people of Israel to the Lord their God. And he will go on before the Lord, in the spirit and power of Elijah, to turn the hearts of the parents to their children and the disobedient to the wisdom of the righteous—to make ready a people prepared for the Lord.'"

Luke 1:23-25: "When his time of service was completed, Zechariah returned home. After this his wife Elizabeth became pregnant and for five months remained in seclusion. 'The Lord has done this for me,' she said. 'In these days he has shown his favor and taken away my disgrace among the people.'"

Luke 1:39-45: "At that time Mary (who became the mother of Jesus) got ready and hurried to a town in the hill country of Judea, where she entered Zechariah's home and greeted Elizabeth. When Elizabeth heard Mary's greeting, the baby leaped in her womb, and Elizabeth was filled with the Holy Spirit. In a loud voice she exclaimed: 'Blessed are you among women, and blessed is the child you will bear! But why am I so favored, that the mother of my Lord should come to me? As soon as the sound of your greeting reached my ears, the baby in my womb leaped for joy. Blessed is she who has believed that the Lord would fulfill his promises to her!'"

To Zechariah and Elizabeth it seemed like a delay or denial of their prayers but in heaven, it was just a logistical issue. The son of Elizabeth had been destined to be the forerunner of our Lord Jesus Christ. Until Mary was chosen by the Almighty and ready for her own role, Elizabeth could not have a child.

What Do You Do If You Suspect The Answers To Your Prayers Are Being Delayed Due To Inappropriate Timing?

In order to prevent a lifetime of heartache and misery, one thing to do in this case is to pray a special type of prayer called a "prayer of enquiry". An enquiry prayer is not a prayer where you ask God to solve a particular problem or challenge. It is a prayer where you seek God's face for direction on what course of action to take or to know his mind concerning a particular issue.

There was a time in the Bible when the Amalekites raided Ziklag in the absence of David and his army. Ziklag was destroyed by fire and all their wives and sons and daughters taken captive - including the family of David. Upon his return, though terribly saddened and distressed, David gathered his strength and decided to pursue the Amalekites to recover all that had been looted away. However, despite his determination and resolve, he wanted to be sure that the outcome would be positive for him and his men and so he offered a prayer of enquiry before taking action.

1 Samuel 30:8: "And David inquired of the Lord, 'Shall I pursue this raiding party? Will I overtake them?' 'Pursue them,' He answered. 'You will certainly overtake them and succeed in the rescue.'"

1 Samuel 30:18-19: "David recovered everything the Amalekites had taken, including his two wives. Nothing was missing: young or old, boy or girl, plunder or anything else they had taken. David brought everything back."

Therefore, if you suspect that answers to prayers are being delayed because of inappropriate timing, pray enquiry prayers to confirm what the situation is from the Lord and he will answer you just as he did for David.

D) Delayed Answers Resulting From Lack of Fasting

If you recall the prayer of Daniel for which the angel was dispatched on the first day, there was something Daniel did in addition to praying.

Daniel 10:2-3: "In those days... I ate no pleasant food, no meat or wine came into my mouth, nor did I anoint myself at all, till three whole weeks were fulfilled."

What Daniel did here is a type of fast. Whenever you deny yourself of the normal pleasures of life in order to seek God's face, you have embarked on a fast. So how did the Angel interpret Daniel's action?

Daniel 10:12: "Then he said to me, 'Do not fear, Daniel, for *from the first day* that you set your heart to understand, *and to humble yourself before your God*, your words were heard; and I have come because of your words.'"

The Angel interpreted Daniel's action as humility. No wonder fasting is so powerful. When you deny yourself of what you cannot ordinarily live without because you want to hear from God, you are showing humility and therefore heaven will reward your action with expedited answers.

Let's take a look at one more passage in the bible to thoroughly illustrate this point.

Mark 9:14-20: "And when He came to the disciples, He saw a great multitude around them, and scribes disputing with them. Immediately, when they saw Him, all the people were greatly amazed, and running to Him, greeted Him. And He asked the scribes, 'What are you discussing with them?' Then one of the crowd answered and said, 'Teacher, I brought You my son, who has a mute spirit. And wherever it seizes him, it throws him down; he foams at the mouth, gnashes his teeth, and becomes rigid. So I spoke to Your disciples, that they should cast it out, but they could not.' Jesus answered him and said, 'O faithless generation, how long shall I be with you? How long shall I bear with you? Bring him to Me.' Then they brought him to Him. And when he saw Him, immediately the spirit convulsed him, and he fell on the ground and wallowed, foaming at the mouth.'"

Mark 9:21-29: "So He asked his father, 'How long has this been happening to him?' And he said, 'From childhood. And often he has thrown him both into the fire and into the water to destroy him. But if You can do anything, have compassion on us and help us.' Jesus said to him, 'If you can believe, all things are possible to him who believes.' Immediately the father of the child cried out and said with tears, 'Lord, I believe; help my unbelief!' When Jesus saw that the people came running together, He rebuked the unclean spirit, saying to it: 'Deaf and dumb spirit, I command you, come out of him and enter him no more!' Then the spirit cried out, convulsed him greatly, and came out of him. And he became as one dead, so that many said, 'He is dead.' But Jesus took him by the hand and lifted him up, and he arose. And when He had come into the house, His disciples asked Him privately, 'Why could we not cast it out?' So He said to them, 'This kind can come out by nothing but *prayer and fasting*.'"

As you can see, some situations respond to nothing but "prayer and fasting".

What Do You Do If You Suspect The Answers To Your Prayers Are Being Delayed Due To Lack of Fasting?

No matter how long you've been praying about some type of problems, until you embark on a fast (which you have seen can be accounted to you for humility), you may experience an answer delay or denial. Prepare yourself to combine fasting with your prayers so as to improve your chance of getting an answer.

Please see chapter 3 for practical information on carrying out a fast.

E) Delayed Answers Resulting From Sin

Isaiah 59:1-2: "Behold, the Lord's hand is not shortened,

that it cannot save; Nor His ear heavy, that it cannot hear. But your iniquities have separated you from your God; And your sins have hidden His face from you, So that He will not hear."

John 9:31: "Now we know that God does not hear sinners; but if anyone is a worshiper of God and does His will, He hears him."

Psalm 34:15-16: "The eyes of the Lord are on the righteous, and his ears are attentive to their cry; but the face of the Lord is against those who do evil, to blot out their name from the earth."

The final reason we will consider in this chapter for delayed or denied answers to prayers is sin. If you are a sinner, except for a prayer of forgiveness, God will not answer your prayer.

What Do You Do If You Suspect The Answers To Your Prayers Are Being Delayed Due To Sin?

Confess your sins and repent, that is, forsake or abandon them. Don't go back to them. After you have done this, you are qualified to pray and God will listen to you. For more on this, please see chapter 3.

In this chapter we have been able to look at a good number of factors that can determine the speed with which you will get answers to your prayers. I am confident that if you follow the content of this chapter carefully and prayerfully as well as the content in the rest of this book, the Almighty will open the windows of heaven and release to you that thing which you are seeking in Jesus name.

3

AM I QUALIFIED TO GET
MY PRAYERS ANSWERED?

In every country in the world, qualifications are a fact of life. Without the proper qualifications, there are certain benefits that you might never get. For example, to get into some colleges or graduate programs, you need to meet or exceed the qualification standards set by the school you are applying to, otherwise your application will be rejected. To become a model and feature in advertisements on TV, radio, magazines or on the internet, you need to have an attractive face or good bodily figure or a good voice. You need all sorts of qualifications for getting employment in banks, research laboratories, factories and all other kinds of businesses.

Furthermore, there are many municipal, state or federal programs for which all "citizens" of every country are eligible. Benefits or programs vary from country to country mainly based on the size of the economy or because a country has adopted a certain ideology or style of government. People qualify for these programs and benefits just by virtue of being citizens of their country. For example, university tuition in nordic countries (Sweden, Finland, Denmark, Norway and Iceland) is completely free to all citizens. No citizen pays anything for tuition.

In the example above, if university education is very important to you and it is not free in your own country and neither can you afford it, you might seriously consider becoming a citizen of a country that offers such a benefit. In order for a foreigner from any country to enjoy the benefits of citizenship of a particular country, he or she must make the appropriate effort to meet the qualification criteria for citizenship set by the country of his or her choice.

Each country has its own requirements for citizenship. For example, certain countries require foreigners to attain a certain level of academic achievement or possess a specific set of skills. Some countries also require you to have spent a certain amount of time (without citizenship benefits) in their country before applying for citizenship. Yet still, there are countries that set a price on citizenship. In these countries, you only need to make payment and satisfy some other requirements.

After meeting the criteria, you are assigned citizenship, made to observe certain rites and then you are issued a passport of that country. With this, you are now fully qualified to receive all the benefits available to citizens of that country without exemption.

In the same vein, the kingdom of God is an entity that requires citizenship. All citizens in this kingdom enjoy very may benefits. One of the most important benefits of kingdom citizenship is the ability to get answers to prayers.

Jeremiah 29:12: "Then you will call on me and come and pray to me, and I will listen to you."

Psalm 91:15: "He will call on me, and I will answer him; I will be with him in trouble, I will deliver him and honor him."

John 16:24: "Until now you have not asked for anything in my name. Ask and you will receive, and your joy will be complete."

John 15:7: "If you remain in me and my words remain in you, ask whatever you wish, and it will be done for you."

Matthew 18:18: "Verily I say unto you, Whatsoever ye shall bind on earth shall be bound in heaven: and whatsoever ye shall loose on earth shall be loosed in heaven."

1 John 5:14-15: "This is the confidence we have in approaching God: that if we ask anything according to his will, he hears us. And if we know that he hears us— whatever we ask—we know that we have what we asked of him."

What a remarkable benefit! There is no other country on earth that offers such a benefit. There is no world leader, congress or parliament or constitution that says to its citizens ask the government anything you want, and as far as it is good and you are eligible for it, it will be given to you! No country on earth regardless of the size of its economy can afford to make such a promise.

Since the Kingdom of God offers you this benefit of answered prayers and if you are interested in something like that, wouldn't you want to know how to qualify to receive such benefits? For anyone interested, the rest of this chapter is focused on exactly how to meet the qualification requirements for answered prayers.

Fortunately, the procedure to qualify for answered prayers is no where near the citizenship requirements of many countries. Qualifying is simple. The following are the necessary steps you need to take. After you have done everything on the list below, you would become a citizen of the Kingdom of God and you would be completely qualified to receive answers to your prayers.

1. Give your Life to Jesus Christ

The first step is to give your life to Jesus Christ. Doing this is very simple. The easiest way to understand what it means to give your life is to recall your relationship with your spouse or someone you are in a committed relationship with. When you are married, you have essentially given your life and your body to your spouse, so to speak. Despite this however, the husband and the wife are still individuals. The husband might have some thoughts or take some actions that he might not share with his wife and vice versa.

When you give your life to Jesus Christ, there is a difference. The action is total. You completely surrender your thoughts, your deeds, spirit, soul and body to Jesus for him to govern. In return, you get all the benefits of kingdom - He will take up responsibility for your daily life, your protection and the protection of your possessions, He will fill your mind with wisdom and understanding, be responsible for your health, He will answer your prayers and He will give you an assurance of eternal life.

Usually, a human being will be bothered about being totally responsible for another person's well-being but not the Lord Jesus Christ.

John 3:16: "For God so loved the world that He gave His one and only Son, that whoever believes in Him shall not perish but have eternal life."

John 6:37: "Whoever comes to me I will never drive away."

John 1:12: "Yet to all who did receive Him, to those who believed in His name, He gave the right to become children of God"

1 Peter 5:7: "Cast all your anxiety on Him because he cares for you."

Revelation 3:20: "Here I am! I stand at the door and knock. If anyone hears my voice and opens the door, I will come in and eat with that person, and they with me."

Romans 10:9: "If you declare with your mouth, 'Jesus is Lord,' and believe in your heart that God raised Him from the dead, you will be saved."

Romans 10:10: "For it is with your heart that you believe and are justified, and it is with your mouth that you profess your faith and are saved."

If you are ready to give your life to Jesus, just read these words both in your spirit and with your lips:

"Lord Jesus, I believe that you are the Son of God. I believe that God sent you to the earth and gave you up to die for my sins. I believe that God raised you from the dead. Today, I give my life to you. Become the Lord of it. All my thoughts and deeds, I lay plain before you. You have said in your word that if I open the door of my life, you will come in. I open my heart to you and I invite you in to come and become the Lord of my life. Thank you for accepting me and giving me the assurance of eternal life."

With those words spoken in your spirit and confessed with your mouth, you have given your life to Jesus Christ. You are now what is known as a Born-again christian.

2. Acknowledge and confess all your sins to Jesus

The next thing you need to do is to admit that you are a sinner and then confess all your sins to the Lord. You are not alone in this. Everyone on earth who is now a believer in Jesus and everyone who is in heaven today were once sinners. The Bible says in Romans 3:23 "For all have sinned and fall short of the glory of God."

In order to be declared righteous and acceptable before God, confession is necessary. 1 John 1:19: "If we confess our sins, he is faithful and just and will forgive us our sins and purify us from all unrighteousness."

Also in order to have true prosperity on the earth, we need to confess our sins. Proverbs 28:13: "Whoever conceals their sins does not prosper."

In the privacy of your room or closet, make a complete mental list of all your sins, admit each one of them and confess them to the Almighty. Then ask Him to forgive you of all your sins.

3. Repent from all confessed sins

After making your confession, the next step is to repent or "forsake" or abandon those sins. That is, do not go back to those sins anymore.

You need to repent because it is a requirement of the kingdom of God. Acts 17:30: "In the past God overlooked such ignorance, but now he commands all people everywhere to repent."

Repentance from sin is also deliverance from spiritual death. Romans 6:23 "For the wages of sin is death, but the gift of God is eternal life in Christ Jesus our Lord." Ezekiel 18:27 "But if a wicked person turns away from the wickedness they have committed and does what is just and right, they will save their life."

Not repenting or forsaking your sins will prevent your prayers from being answered. This runs counter to your primary objective in this book. Psalm 66:18: "If I had cherished sin in my heart, the Lord would not have listened."

Let's be plain, if a person is sent to jail for carjacking and is released after serving some time, then after the release goes and does it again, the fact that he has served time for the first crime does not preclude him from being thrown in jail again. The situation is the same with sin. Repentance means that you stop sinning in order to enjoy to God's benefits - in this case, answers to your prayers.

4. Forgive others who have offended you

One of the major qualifications for getting your prayers answered is to forgive and release people who have offended you. Jesus highlighted this when He was teaching His disciples how to pray. The prayer referred to as the Lord's Prayer, has a line it that says "And forgive us our debts, as we also have forgiven our debtors." (Matthew 6:12).

The word 'debt' above is in reference to sin as we can see in Matthew 6:14-15: "For if you forgive other people when they sin against you, your heavenly Father will also forgive you. But if you do not forgive others their sins, your Father will not forgive your sins."

God will not forgive you your sins if you do not forgive others. This means no benefits, meaning there will be no answer to your prayer unless you forgive.

This issue of forgiving others was so central to the message of Christ while He was on earth that He decided to further expound on the issue in what is now popularly called the "Parable of the Unforgiving servant."

Here is the parable in its entirety:

Matthew 18:23-27: "Therefore, the kingdom of heaven is like a king who wanted to settle accounts with his servants. As he began the settlement, a man who owed him ten thousand bags of gold was brought to him. Since he was not able to pay, the master ordered that he and his wife and his children and all that he had be sold to repay the debt. 'At this the servant fell on his knees before him. 'Be patient with me,' he begged, 'and I will pay back everything.' The servant's master took pity on him, canceled the debt and let him go."

Matthew 18:28-32: "But when that servant went out, he found one of his fellow servants who owed him a hundred silver coins. He grabbed him and began to choke him. 'Pay back what you owe me!' he demanded. 'His fellow servant fell to his knees and begged him, 'Be patient with me, and I will pay it back.' "But he refused. Instead, he went off and had the man thrown into prison until he could pay the debt. When the other servants saw what had happened, they were outraged and went and told their master everything that had happened. 'Then the master called the servant in. 'You wicked servant,' he said, 'I canceled all that debt of yours because you begged me to. Shouldn't you have had mercy on your fellow servant just as I had on you?' In anger his master handed him over to the jailers to be tortured, until he should pay back all he owed."

Matthew 18:35: "This is how my heavenly Father will treat each of you unless you forgive your brother or sister from your heart."

Without forgiving other people who have offended you, it is not possible to get an answer to your prayers from God.

5. Start, and develop a relationship with Jesus

If you need answered prayers from God, you need to develop a good relationship with Jesus. John 14:6: "I am the way and the truth and the life. No one comes to the Father except through me." This is why we pray in Jesus name.

Developing a relationship with God involves getting to know Him. There is no better way to do that than to get a Bible and start reading it. This might be very simple for some but difficult for others. In this case, you can find encouragement and enlightenment by asking around for or by yourself locating a church whose principles are based on the Bible. The Bible even encourages this. Hebrews 10:24-25: 'And let us consider how we may spur one another on toward love and good deeds, not giving up meeting together, as some are in the habit of doing, but encouraging one another.'"

Do not delay. Begin this relationship today.

6. Develop Faith in God

Another thing that qualifies you to receive answers to your prayers is Faith. Exhibiting faith simply means that you believe that God is for real and that He will do that thing which you have asked of Him. Hebrews 11:1 "Now faith is confidence in what we hope for and assurance about what we do not see." This is one thing that really pleases God and moves Him to act on your behalf. Hebrews 11:6 "And without faith it is impossible to please God, because anyone who comes to him must believe that he exists and that he rewards those who earnestly seek him."

In fact, there is a promise of answered prayers tied

to having faith. Matthew 21:22 "If you believe, you will receive whatever you ask for in prayer."

So anytime you ask anything of God and you cast aside doubt and you believe totally that He will do what you are asking, you are exhibiting faith.

If you are new to the Kingdom of God or even sometimes when you have spent years as a born-again christian, you need to ensure that your ability to exercise faith and therefore receive more answered prayers is at or remains at its peak. There are so many things around us to discourage us and bring down our faith. To develop faith or to maintain it, the only thing you need to do is read or listen to God's word - the Bible and sermons preached by Bible-believing preachers. The Bible says in Romans 10:17 "Consequently, faith comes from hearing the message, and the message is heard through the word about Christ."

The word of God is the source of faith. That is the only place it comes from. The less of it you read, listen to or watch, the less faith you will have and the fewer answered prayers you will get. The more of the word of God that goes into you, the more answered prayers you will get.

7. Fasting

This is an optional qualification for answers prayers. It is not exactly required all the time to get your prayers answered. But as we saw in Chapter 2, there are certain prayers that will never be answered except you pray and fast at the same time. In that chapter, we looked at the example of Daniel when he embarked on a fast at the same time he was praying to understand why the children of God were still in bondage after the seventy years of prophesied slavery had elapsed. We also looked at the example of the disciples of Jesus who had struggled and failed to cast out a demon from a boy until Jesus came and cast it out in a few seconds. In the same passage, Jesus said "This kind [of demon] can come out by nothing but prayer and fasting."

Fasting is essentially denying yourself of pleasure especially food and drink for a given time sufficient enough to make you humble in spirit, soul and body.

Since fasting is such a powerful tool, you might ask the question "how do I fast?" This section provides you with examples of fasting from the Bible.

a) The Three Day Fast without food and drink

Esther 4:16 "Go, gather together all the Jews who are in Susa, and fast for me. Do not eat or drink for three days, night or day. I and my attendants will fast as you do. When this is done, I will go to the king, even though it is against the law. And if I perish, I perish"

Haman was an influential advisor to King Ahasuerus of Persia who had recently married Esther, a jew. Haman had plotted to destroy all jews as soon as possible. If he succeeded, it would mean Esther herself would also die. In the above passage, after reviewing the consequence of appearing before the King without being summoned, Esther called for a fast as she approached the King to expose and foil Haman's plan. The fast was to last for three days and nights and there was to be no food or water during the three day period. God honored the fasting and prayer because all the jews were spared. It did not end there, Haman, the evil plotter was killed in place of the jews. Plus, the King gave Esther everything that Haman had owned. Talk about a resounding answer to prayer with extra benefits!

Depending on how serious your problem is, you can adopt this fasting regimen. This means you will not eat or drink anything for three days and for every day of the three days, you will need to set aside time to pray. Fasting without praying is merely a self-imposed hunger strike.

Also do not forget to read the word of God for everyday of the fast. Remember that faith comes by reading, hearing, watching or listening to the word of God.

b) The Twenty One Day Fast without sweet food or drinks

To properly illustrate this, let's revisit the passage we looked at in Chapter 2.

Daniel 10:2-3: "At that time I, Daniel, mourned for three weeks. I ate no choice food; no meat or wine touched my lips; and I used no lotions at all until the three weeks were over."

After Daniel finished the fast, this is what happened:

Daniel 10:10-12: "A hand touched me and set me trembling on my hands and knees. He said, "Daniel, you who are highly esteemed, consider carefully the words I am about to speak to you, and stand up, for I have now been sent to you." And when he said this to me, I stood up trembling. Then he continued, "Do not be afraid, Daniel. Since the first day that you set your mind to gain understanding and to humble yourself before your God, your words were heard, and I have come in response to them."

The twenty one day fasting and prayer program Daniel embarked on provoked the physical appearance of an angel to deliver the answer. According to the passage, the fasting was interpreted by Heaven as a "humbling of himself before God."

So how did he do it? During the twenty days, he did not eat any "choice" food, no meat, no wine and he did not use any lotions on his body. If you decide to adopt Daniel's fast, you will also have to do likewise. You will need to cut out for twenty one days, any food you consider to be delicious or drink you consider to be tasty and eat only basic food in small quantities and essentially drink only water.

As with the three day fast, you must set aside a particular time each day to read the word of God (for faith) and to pray.

Finally, before adopting and embarking on any of the featured fasting and prayer program examples described above, it is advisable to consult your doctor to confirm whether or not you are fit enough to do the fast. This is quite important.

4

PREPARING YOURSELF FOR PRAYERS
(CHAPTER INCLUDES ACTIVITIES TO BE DONE DAILY OR EACH TIME BEFORE PRAYERS)

Before praying the prayers in Chapter 5, you should read the scriptures, bible confessions and personal affirmations in this chapter. You should also sing all the songs contained in this chapter. Only after finishing these activities should you proceed to pray the Open Heavens prayers in Chapter 5.

When we pray, the answers we expect are sent to us from heaven. When God answers prayer, the answer descends from heaven unto the earth. And surely God answers prayers. Philippians 4:19 - "And my God will meet all your needs according to the riches of his glory in Christ Jesus."

Heaven, in this context is like an interface between the heaven in which God resides and the earth, where humans exist. The easiest analogue to this is the internet browser, that is, the piece of software that allows you to access the internet. If you are in your home or office and you have the desire to purchase a book or other item on the internet, you need to get to the online store selling that item through a browser. If everything is okay, you "open" the browser, visit the store, place your order and you either download the item or it arrives at your doorsteps hours or days later.

However, there are times when problems can occur with this process. For example, your internet connection is bad and as such the browser is unable to mediate the process. Again, it could be that while browsing some malicious websites, a piece of malware had been installed in your computer with the same effect - a lack of access. In some cases, there is nothing wrong with the internet connection or the browser but the online store has decided that people who live outside or in certain countries should be automatically blocked from using their store. One other problem is not knowing how to use the computer and the browser at all in the first place. Whatever the reason, the consequence is that you cannot access what you desire.

This is how it is with answered prayers as well.

People who pray and receive answers from God, have Open Heavens over them whereas people who pray and do not receive any answer from God have Closed Heavens over their lives. It is a tragedy to have the heavens closed to you. Apart from not getting answers to prayers, it means you are effectively cut off from the creator of the heavens and the earth. What could be worse than that?

If you have read Chapters 1 - 3, you should not have a problem with your heavens being open at this point for most of the reasons given in our browser example. However, the final example given is not knowing how to use the computer or browser in the first place. The rest of this book is dedicated to making sure you know exactly how to access heaven and get your prayers answered.

HEAVEN IS AN INTERFACE FOR PRAYER

Genesis 28:10-14: "Jacob left Beersheba and set out for Harran. When he reached a certain place, he stopped for the night because the sun had set. Taking one of the stones there, he put it under his head and lay down to sleep. *He had a dream in which he saw a stairway resting on the earth, with its top reaching to heaven, and the angels of God were ascending and descending on it.* There above it stood the Lord, and he said: "I am the Lord, the God of your father Abraham and the God of Isaac. I will give you and your descendants the land on which you are lying. Your descendants will be like the dust of the earth, and you will spread out to the west and to the east, to the north and to the south. All peoples on earth will be blessed through you and your offspring."

There is a spiritual stairway with its foot on the earth and the top in heaven. Some scholars have said that, amongst other things, the angels ascending are taking people's prayers into heaven whereas the ones descending are returning with answered prayers. So you can see clearly that the heavens are an interface for you and I to use to access the Almighty for any purpose according to His will.

CLOSED HEAVENS

Unfortunately, as earlier hinted, sometimes the heavens can be closed or shut against people. When this happens, you cannot get any answer from or engage in any other form of communication with God.

2 Chronicles 7:13-14 - "When I shut up the heavens so that there is no rain, or command locusts to devour the land or send a plague among my people, if my people, who are called by my name, will humble themselves and pray and seek my face and turn from their wicked ways, then I will hear from heaven, and I will forgive their sin and will heal their land." - with remedy.

Luke 4:25-26 - "I assure you that there were many widows in Israel in Elijah's time, when the sky was shut for three and a half years and there was a severe famine throughout the land..."

This is not a situation anyone wants to be in. If a person has closed heavens over them and you have read and carried out everything in chapters 1 - 3, the only other reason for a closed heaven will be a lack of knowhow to access heaven and this is what we address in chapter 5. As mentioned, you might have a healthy computer and an excellent internet connection but if you do not know how to use it, you cannot make a successful transaction.

OPEN HEAVENS

A) The Heavens can open as a direct result of God's grace

Deuteronomy 28:12 - "The LORD will open the heavens, the storehouse of his bounty, to send rain on your land in season and to bless all the work of your hands. You will lend to many nations but will borrow from none."

Luke 4:25-26 - "I assure you that there were many widows in Israel in Elijah's time, when the sky was shut for three and a half years and there was a severe famine throughout the land. Yet Elijah was not sent to any of them, but to a widow in Zarephath in the region of Sidon."

B) The Heavens can open as a direct answer to prayer

Acts 10:9 - "About noon the following day as they were on their journey and approaching the city, *Peter went up on the roof to pray.* He became hungry and wanted something to eat, and while the meal was being prepared, he fell into a trance. *He saw heaven opened...*"

Isaiah 64:1-2 - "Oh, *that you would rend the heavens and come down,* that the mountains would tremble before you! As when fire sets twigs ablaze and causes water to boil, come down to make your name known to your enemies and cause the nations to quake before you!"

Luke 3:21 - "When all the people were being baptized, Jesus was baptized too. *And as he was praying, heaven was opened* and the Holy Spirit descended on him in bodily form like a dove. And a voice came from heaven: "You are my Son, whom I love; with you I am well pleased."

   2 Chronicles 7:14 - "If my people, who are called by my name, will humble themselves *and pray and seek my face* and turn from their wicked ways, *then I will hear from heaven*, and I will forgive their sin and will heal their land."

   These scriptures give us hope that we can pray for the heavens to open and receive assurance that we will get exactly what we are looking for and even much more.

<u>WORDS OF PRAISE TO GOD</u>

The following praises are to be offered to God before you pray the prayers in Chapter 5. As you say these words, concentrate. Visualize yourself in the presence of the Almighty God and speak to Him with all the sincerity you can muster. Remember, He is the creator of everything that exists including you. He made you and He is the only one that can answer your prayers. No one else can do that beside Him. You can repeat each of the lines three times each or read through the entire list and repeat three times.

1.   There is none like you O God.

2.   You are the King of Kings and Lord of Lords.

3.   You are the most high and I worship you.

4.   You are highly lifted up there is no one is up to you.

5. You are the I am that I am. Lord be lifted high and be glorified forever and ever.

6. Lord I bless you. The sun, moon, and stars praise you.

7. All of creation praises you, oh Lord.

8. All the angels and all of Heaven praise you O Lord.

9. I bow before you because you are Omnipotent, Omniscient and Omnipresent.

10. Lord I adore you because you are all-powerful, you have all knowledge and you are everywhere. My whole trust is in you O God.

11. You are the Alpha and Omega - the beginning and the ending.

12. You are the One who is, the One who was, the One who is to come.

13. Ancient of Days, I praise you.

14. You are the Rock of Ages and there is no one else beside you.

15. I magnify your Holy Name and I adore you O Lord.

16. You are the only one whose love endures forever. I

bless you.

17. You are worthy to be called Wonderful Counselor, Mighty God, Everlasting Father and Prince of Peace.

18. Lord, receive all my praises, glory, honor and adoration.

19. You are a marvellous God. What a mighty God I serve.

20. You are worthy to be praised and you are worthy to be glorified. Be exalted forever oh Lord, in Jesus name.

WORDS OF THANKSGIVING TO GOD

The following thanks are to be offered to God each time before you pray the prayers in Chapter 5. Before you read out these words of thanksgiving, take a moment to thank God for yourself for all the good things He has done for you recently. Think about all these good things. Be plain and thank Him from the bottom of your heart with sincere gratitude. You can repeat each of the lines three times each or read through the entire list and repeat three times.

1. Take a moment and recall every good thing that God has done in your life or in your family in recent times and thank Him for each of those things.

2. Lord, I thank you for your Righteousness, your Holy

Name and your mighty deeds.

3. Father, I thank you for sending your son, the Lord Jesus Christ, to die for my sins.

4. Father, I thank you for raising Him up from the grave and for giving me the assurance of eternal life.

5. I thank you for your marvellous and wondrous works.

6. Thank you Lord because I am fearfully and wonderfully made.

7. I thank you for your counsel upon my life and for the instructions you pass to me even through dreams that guide me in my path.

8. I thank you for the hope I have in you.

9. Lord I thank you for saving my soul and for redeeming me from the fires of hell.

10. Thank you for allowing me into your presence because therein is fullness of joy.

11. Thank you because each time I am in distress and I call upon you, you hearken your ear unto my cry.

12. Thank you for being my strength and for saving me from the hands of my enemies.

13. Thank you for delivering me from trouble and from the hands of death.

14. Thank you for your great and merciful kindness towards me and your compassion upon me.

15. Thank you for loading me with benefits every single day of my life.

16. I thank you for your Power that can never fail.

17. Thank you for your promise to always answer me when I call.

18. Thank you because you are my rock, my fortress and my deliverer. In you I take refuge. You are my shield and the horn of my salvation, my stronghold. I bless you.

19. Thank you for your promise to meet all my needs according to the riches of your glory in Christ Jesus.

20. I bless you oh Lord. Accept all of my thanks and praises in Jesus name.

SONGS OF THANKSGIVING, PRAISE & WORSHIP

The book of Acts 16 makes it clear that Paul and Silas were praying and singing while in bondage before their miraculous deliverance by the Almighty from the jailhouse. There is a strange liberating power in songs and prayer.

Sing each of these thanksgiving and worship songs one or more times before beginning the prayers in chapter 5.

1. Thank You Lord
(For sing-along video and lyrics, see https://www.youtube.com/watch?v=K44trVhtZX4)

2. Lord, I Give You My Heart
(For sing-along video and lyrics, see, https://www.youtube.com/watch?v=mZGzu6oI9b4)

3. As We Worship You
(For sing-along video and lyrics, see, https://www.youtube.com/watch?v=hKbmjI_XTfM)

4. God Is Good
(For sing-along video and lyrics, see, https://www.youtube.com/watch?v=Jl06RN5zRxk)

SONGS OF PRAYER
The book of Acts 16 makes it clear that Paul and Silas were praying and singing while in bondage before their miraculous deliverance by the Almighty from the jailhouse. There is a strange liberating power in songs and prayer. Sing each of these prayer songs one or more times before beginning the prayers in chapter 5.

1. Our Father Who Art In Heaven
(For sing-along video and lyrics, see, https://www.youtube.com/watch?v=lUkAzyDRL5E)

2. God Will Make A Way Where There Seems To Be No Way

(For sing-along video and lyrics, see, https://www.youtube.com/watch?v=1zo3fJYtS-o)

3. If We Call To Him

(For sing-along video and lyrics, see, https://www.youtube.com/watch?v=YwdrxstwPvo)

4. The Promise

(For sing-along video and lyrics, see, https://www.youtube.com/watch?v=ursASAdsipI)

5. Nothing Is Impossible With God

(For sing-along video and lyrics, see,, https://www.youtube.com/watch?v=rips2XpzkjE)

5

BREAKTHROUGH PRAYERS FOR STARTUPS & ENTREPRENEURS

If you have read chapters 1 - 4 and you've done everything written therein, you should now have full confidence that if you pray, God will answer your prayers. Like we have seen elsewhere in this book, God does not withhold any good thing from His children. You are now a child of God and since starting a new business is a good thing, he will not withhold it from you. The prayers in this chapter are the ones that will open heavens for you and get you what you need — a successful business. Have absolute faith in God. If you do not yet have faith, go re-read previous chapters in this book that highlight people who got their prayers answered. Then go into the Bible for yourself to read about more people who God heard their prayers. After that, go online, watch videos and listen to testimonies of people who are alive and well and for whom God has done miracles. Then, when your faith is built up, return here to pray these prayers. As surely as there is a God in heaven, He will answer you and you will have your own testimony in the mighty name of Jesus.

PRAYERS OF ENQUIRY FROM THE ALMIGHTY

1 Samuel 30:8-9 "And David inquired of the Lord, 'Shall I pursue this raiding party? Will I overtake them?' 'Pursue them,' he answered. 'You will certainly overtake them and succeed in the rescue.'" Proverbs 3:5-5 "Trust in the Lord with all your heart and lean not on your own understanding; in all your ways submit to him, and he will make your paths straight." This section of prayers is for those who want to hear from God before going into a particular business.

1. Heavenly Father, according to your word, I have come to seek your face today. Answer me, in the name of Jesus.

2. O Lord my God, as I begin to pray right now, hearken unto my voice and answer me in the name of Jesus.

3. Father Lord, your word says in Proverbs 16:9 "A man's heart plans his way, But the Lord directs his steps." I have made my plans, O Lord, hear me and direct my steps in the name of Jesus.

3. Father Lord, I present the business of _____ before you. Should I go into this business or not?
   [*Replace the gap in the prayer point with the name of the business you want to go into*]

4. Father, visit me in my dream and provide me with an answer of peace on this matter, in the name of Jesus.

5. Almighty God, use a vision of the day time to show me which way to go in the name of Jesus.

6. Lord God, use human beings who have never heard of my plans as a channel to confirm your answer to me, in the name of Jesus.

7. Lord God, if I go into the business of _____, will I prosper in it? Answer me O lord, in the name of Jesus.

8. Lord Jesus, if I go into the business of _____, will you back me all the way? Answer me O Lord in the name of Jesus.

9. Father, send your divine angels to me to give me an answer of peace on this matter, in the name of Jesus.

10. My Father, use anything or anybody to confirm your answer to me, in the name of Jesus.

11. O Lord, I pray, if you have not destined me to do the business of _____ , help me O Lord, and show me what business you want for my destiny, in the name of Jesus.

12. My God, if the business of _____ is not what you have planned for me, then O Lord, that business that you have attached to my destiny from the beginning of time, reveal it unto me, in the name of Jesus.

13. I reject the spirit of error. By your grace O Lord, I will not make the mistake that will cause me pain and lead me to regret, in the name of Jesus.

14. Today, I decree that I receive divine guidance to go into business. I receive the power to make wealth. I shall prosper and I shall fulfill my destiny. It is well with me, in the mighty name of Jesus.

PRAYERS TO OBTAIN POWER TO DO BUSINESS

Deuteronomy 8:18 "But remember the Lord your God, for it is he who gives you the ability to produce wealth." The ability to do business and to trade comes from God. If you want to go into business and you lack the ability to do business or you require fortification of your ability, these are the prayers you need to pray.

1. Almighty and everlasting Father, give me a curious and creative mind so I can use it to create products and services that people will patronize, in the name of Jesus.

2. O Lord, build up in me a natural desire to locate pertinent problems and provide solutions that can lead to a business, in the name of Jesus.

3. Father Lord, imbue me with an undying desire to buy and sell, in the name of Jesus.

4. Everlasting Father, give me unusual wisdom that will give me business success, in the name of Jesus.

5. O Lord, anoint me with the oil of favor. Whenever I come in contact with people that will advance my business, let them favor me, in the name of Jesus.

6. O Lord, send people my way that will provide me with information that will advance the cause of my business in the name of Jesus.

7. Strange but anointed ideas that can develop into successful businesses, enter into my life now, in the name of Jesus.

8. O Lord, by your power, cause me to be in the right place, at the right time to hear or to see that thing that will make me succeed in business in the name of Jesus.

9. Father Lord, have favor upon and connect me to men and women that will make my business prosper in the name of Jesus.

10. Father Lord, use neighbors (current or former) to link me up to the business that you have decided for my destiny, in the name of Jesus.

11. Lord, convert my co-workers (current or former) into channels of blessing for my business, in the name of Jesus.

12. Almighty God, use my friends and schoolmates as

instruments to link me up with the business you have destined for me, in the name of Jesus.

13. Father, plant the thought of helping me into the minds of any man or woman that can help me with my business in the name of Jesus. Let them never rest until thy locate me, in the name of Jesus.

14. O Lord, take the money that I have to start this business and multiply it for me, in the name of Jesus. As you multiplied that boy's five loaves and two fishes to feed five thousand, O Lord, by your miraculous power, multiply my capital also so it can be sufficient to fund my business, in the name of Jesus.

15. Father Lord, remove all the limitations that will prevent me from prospering in business, in the name of Jesus.

16. Any natural trait that does not go along with business in me, O Lord, remove it in the name of Jesus.

17. Lord Jesus, imbue with enthusiasm that can attract customers, in the name of Jesus.

18. Lord, as you provided Jacob with unusual wisdom in his dealings with Laban, miraculously provide me with the wisdom that will prosper my business, in the name of Jesus.

19. Father, as I begin the process of developing my product, O Lord, give me the mental fortitude to keep experimenting until I have perfected my product and service, in the name of Jesus.

20. I reject every spirit of discouragement. I refuse to be discouraged. I will achieve my goals and my business will work, in the name of Jesus.

21. As I enter into this business, anything I am sacrificing right now - my money, my time, certain relationships, O Lord, by your power, I shall gain them back multiple fold in the name of Jesus.

22. I convert every ridicule or mockery directed my way by detractors into motivational vitamins, in the name of Jesus.

23. Jehovah, as I go about to meet experts that can teach me about the business I want to go into, O Lord, give me favor before them, in the name of Jesus.

24. Lord Jesus, do not let any expert or consultant take advantage of my lack of knowledge, in the name of Jesus. Lead me to the right experts and consultants, in the name of Jesus.

25. Where I will establish my business, O Lord, reveal unto me, in the name of Jesus.

26. Father, let me establish my business in the place where I will receive maximum exposure and customers will locate me in the name of Jesus.

27. Father, you are the one that blesses and adds no sorrow. As I take this step to go into business, bless me indeed and do not let me experience sorrow on this journey, in the name of Jesus.

28. Today, I decree that I receive divine guidance to go into business. I receive the power to make wealth. I shall prosper and I shall fulfill my destiny. It is well with me, in the mighty name of Jesus.

PRAYERS TO PROFIT IN BUSINESS
Isaiah 48:17 "I am the Lord your God, Who teaches you to profit, Who leads you by the way you should go." This section is for those who desire to obtain profit for their hard work and business. God can teach you to profit in ways that will make you a wonder in your generation.

1. Heavenly Father, inspire me to create products and services that people have been looking for, in the name of Jesus.

2. Lord Jesus, lead me to the place where I will find the materials I need for my business at the best quality for the lowest price so that I can make profit, in the make of Jesus.

3. Father Lord, convert people I know and people I do

not know into channels of advertisement for my business, in the name of Jesus.

4. Father Lord, use divinely orchestrated accidents to lead me to create products and services that people need in the name of Jesus.

5. Lord, give me divine favor before people in the name of Jesus. In the marketplace, let people prefer my products or services above that of any other person, in the name of Jesus.

6. I pray, Lord God of heaven, that nothing will cause me to bring down the quality of my products and services in the name of Jesus.

7. O Lord God, send my way, employees that will be a plus to my business, in the name of Jesus.

8. Lord Jesus, inspire men and women, boys and girls who have profitable ideas to come and work for me or with me in the name of Jesus.

9. Father, bless the ideas of my employees. Whenever they suggest them and we carry them out, let them lead to profit for the business, in the name of Jesus.

10. By your miraculous power O Lord, reveal unto me the strategies of my competitors so that i can continue to stay ahead, in the name of Jesus.

11. Father, teach me to manage and expand my business in such a way that it will continue to remain profitable in the name of Jesus.

12. Wherever any material I need that can boost the profitability of my business is located, Father, send men and women to reveal information about the material to me so I can profit from it in the name of Jesus.

13. Hear me O Lord, bless me with the unusual ability to create certain products and services that no one else can do, in the name of Jesus.

14. Teach me O Lord to market my products and services in the right place and to the right people, i the name of Jesus.

15. Lord, I ask you to take charge of my life. Any human flaw in me that can negatively affect my business, remove it form my life in the name of Jesus.

16. Father Lord, any flaw in the lives of my workers or partners that can negatively affect my life, remove it from them so that my business will not suffer in the name of Jesus.

17. Teach me O Lord to always price my products and services so that it is the best for my customers, in the name of Jesus.

18. Almighty God, if my business is located in the wrong place for the type of business I'm doing and is therefore affecting my profitability, reveal this to me so I can relocate, in the name of Jesus.

19. Lord, provide me with all the information and materials to provide the best possible products and services in the name of Jesus.

20. O great and awesome God, inspire me to create the best available products and services so that people will be falling over themselves to patronize me, in the name of Jesus.

21. Father Lord, cause people who have used my products and services in the past to recommend me to people they know and those that they do not know, in the name of Jesus.

22. Now, Lord, when I go to submit my products with a distributor, give me favor before them, in the name of Jesus.

23. Father, let distributors take me products far and wide so I can make maximum profit, in the name of Jesus.

24. As my products are added to the channels of my distributor, let people locate them and fall in love with them, in the name of Jesus.

25. I decree that it is well with me and I will make it in the name of Jesus.

26. The hand of the Almighty will be permanently on my business so that it shall prosper, in the name of Jesus.

27. In amazing ways, the Almighty will teach me how to prosper, according to His word and I will not suffer loss in the name of Jesus.

28. The Lord will anoint me with the oil of gladness above my fellows. I shall prosper far and beyond all of my competitors in every marketplace because the Lord is with me, in the name of Jesus.

29. O great and awesome God, use me as an example to demonstrate your power of favor, in the name of Jesus.

30. Today, I decree that I receive divine guidance to go into business. I receive the power to make wealth. I shall prosper and I shall fulfill my destiny. It is well with me, in the mighty name of Jesus.

PRAYERS OF PROTECTION FROM BUSINESS LOSS

Operating a business with no revenue is bad. Running a business that makes losses is even worse. It can push you into debt and incurring debts could have several negative consequences on your life that go beyond just your business. The Almighty can protect you against loss in your business. These are the prayers you need to pray if you desire this type of protection.

1. Father, if I am in the wrong business already, reveal this to me so I can drop it, in the name of Jesus.

2. Lord, by your mighty power, reveal unto me any plans of my competitors and detractors to bring down my business, in the name of Jesus.

3. O Lord, cause me to lose interest in signing any document that has been designed to put me and my business in bondage, in the name of Jesus.

4. I will not make any unfortunate mistake that will put my business in jeopardy, in the name of Jesus.

5. My colleagues and employees will not make any mistake that will put my business in jeopardy in the name of Jesus.

6. Any conspiracy that is being hatched or that will be hatched against me and my business, as with the example of Haman, let it be frustrated in the name of Jesus.

7. Lord, my products will not lose their quality, in the name of Jesus.

8. Most High God, by your grace, my business will not catch fire, in the name of Jesus.

9. I shall not be involved in any accident that will harm me, in the name of Jesus.

10. My colleagues and employees will not be involved in any accident that will harm them in the name of Jesus.

11. I shall not die neither shall my employees die in the name of Jesus.

12. I reject any sickness that might come to derail my business, in the name of Jesus.

13. My family members will not fall into any sickness that can negatively affect my business, in the name of Jesus.

14. Lord, let your mark be upon my business. It shall not become a victim of any kind of theft, in the name of Jesus.

15. My products and services will not be rejected wherever I present them for sale or distribution in the name of Jesus.

16. My products or serves will not be removed from anywhere where they are currently being sold or offered in the name of Jesus.

17. Bad weather shall not ruin my business, in the name of Jesus.

18. Regardless of what type of economy we are in, my business shall continue to experience prosperity as it was for Joseph in the land of Egypt, in the name of Jesus.

19. I shall suffer no loss.

20. Today, It is well with me, with family and with my business. I decree that I receive divine guidance to go into business. I receive the power to make wealth. I shall prosper and I shall fulfill my destiny. It is well with me, in the mighty name of Jesus.

PRAYERS AGAINST NEGATIVE SPIRITUAL FORCES

Powers of darkness can be deployed against a business for a variety of reasons. Businesses that suffer from attacks of this kind will make slow progress or will not make any progress at all. If you do not want your business to be a victim of demonic powers, please pray these prayers.

1. Hear me O Lord and encircle me with the wall of fire, in the name of Jesus.

2. I frustrate any attack of the devil on my business, in

the name of Jesus.

3. By the power in the blood of Jesus, I frustrate the efforts of any evil competitor that wants my business to die so that his or hers can prosper. Their efforts shall not prosper against me in the name of Jesus.

4. I establish a defensive shield over my life and my family. Let any wicked spiritual arrow fired against my life, my family and my business return to the sender in the name of Jesus.

5. Any power of my father's house, that has seen that my business is prospering and does not want me to excel, be destroyed in the name of Jesus.

6. I reject any satanically spirit of discouragement. I refuse to be discouraged. Instead I shall continue to work harder and prosper, in the name of Jesus.

7. Any power of darkness that has sworn that it is over their dead body that I shall prosper in business, Lord, answer their prayers and let me prosper in the name of Jesus.

8. Any power of darkness attacking my finances in order to attack my business, lose your hold over my life, in the name of Jesus.

9. By the power in the blood of Jesus, I break any evil

curse of darkness that has been issued against my business. Let the reverse of that curse manifest in my life in the name of Jesus.

10. Any man or woman that has been hired to curse my business for any reason, hear me and hear me well, as with the example of Balaam, the Almighty will convert all your curses into blessings for my favor, in the name of Jesus.

11. Any evil physical object such as charms that have been dropped at my place of business in order to attack me or my business, I decree in the name of Jesus, you this physical object of darkness, lose your power, in the name of Jesus.

12. Any sickness fashioned against me by powers of darkness, you shall not prosper, in the name of Jesus. I will not fall sick and my business will not suffer, in the name of Jesus.

13. Any sickness fashioned against members of my family with the purpose of making me spend all my resources and to kill my business, listen up, you shall not prosper in the name of Jesus. No member of my family shall fall victim to demonic sicknesses in the name of Jesus.

14. All arrows of loss, i fire them back to their senders in the name of Jesus.

15. All arrows of backwardness, I send them back to their senders, in the name of Jesus.

16. I decree that it is well with me, with my family members, with my employees and colleagues and with my business, in the name of Jesus.

17. As light overcomes darkness, I shall overcome any attack of the enemy fashioned against me in the name of Jesus.

18. My business will succeed, in the name of Jesus.

19. I shall live well and long to enjoy the fruits of my labor, in the name of Jesus.

20. Today, It is well with me, with family and with my business. I decree that I receive divine guidance to go into business. I receive the power to make wealth. I shall prosper and I shall fulfill my destiny. It is well with me, in the mighty name of Jesus.

THANKSGIVING FOR ANSWERED PRAYERS

In this section, thank God any way you can. Give Him praise for the mighty victory He has won for you. Stay in faith as you await the manifestation of your prayers. God Bless you, in Jesus mighty name!

Stay in faith as you await the manifestation of your prayers. God Bless you, in Jesus mighty name!

Made in the USA
Lexington, KY
26 December 2016